A DEFENCE
OF
HINDOO THEISM
IN REPLY
TO THE ATTACK OF AN ADVOCATE
FOR
IDOLATRY
AT MADRAS

A DEFENCE

OF

HINDOO THEISM

IN REPLY

TO THE ATTACK OF AN ADVOCATE

FOR

IDOLATRY,

AT MADRAS

RAM MOHUN ROY

GYAN

Published by

GYAN

Gyan Publishing House
5, Ansari Road
Daryaganj, New Delhi-110002
Phone: 011-47034999, 9811692060
E-mail: books@gyanbooks.com

Distribution Network
gyanbooks.com
India, USA, Canada, UK, Australia

ISBN: 978-93-6920-360-4 (HB)

First Published, 1817

2nd Impression 2025

Printed at: Gyan Press, Delhi.

A DEFENCE OF HINDOO THEISM IN REPLY TO THE ATTACK OF AN ADVOCATE FOR IDOLATRY, AT MADRAS
Author : RAM MOHUN ROY

A DEFENCE

OF

HINDOO THEISM

IN REPLY

TO THE ATTACK OF AN ADVOCATE

FOR

IDOLATRY,

AT MADRAS.

BY

RAM MOHUN ROY.

CALCUTTA.

1817.

PREFACE.

The following sheets contain some remarks in reply to a publication which appeared in the Madras Courier of December last, under the signature of Sankara Sastri, in answer to my abridgment of the vedant and my preface to the translation of the Ishopanishad as well as to my Introduction to the Cenopanishad. The length, to which the arguments of the controvertist extended, having precluded their appearance in the Calcutta prints, I have taken the liberty of reprinting them along with my own observations on them, in order that the discussion may be brought fully before the public, to whose decision the merits of the question must now be left.

TO THE

EDITOR OF THE

MADRAS COURIER.

SIR,

On reading your Peper, dated 19th November 1816, I found a publication in it taken from a Calcutta Paper, respecting the Theological Doctrines of RAM MOHUN ROY, on which I shall proceed to make a few observations.

In the first part of this publication, it is stated "this eminently learned and indefatigable reformer is proceeding, with unremitting exertions, in the laudable work of enlightening his Countrymen, and reclaiming them from their debasing system of Idolatry. Having, for the "instruction of the Hindu population of these "provinces, translated into Bengalese the prin- "cipal chapters of the Veds, he has now done "a few of them into English for the grati- "fication of such European Gentlemen as in- "terest themselves in the improvement of their "fellow-creatures."

In a former paper, also, it was stated that the learned person here mentioned, had "*discovered*" that the Doctrine of the Unity of the God-head was taught in the Puránas and Tantras as well as the Vedas.

The worship of the All-pervading and Supreme Being is the original doctrine founded on the Vedas, Purnas, &c. and is known in general in this, as well as in the other parts of the Peninsula:—this faith is known by the name of *Adwaitam*, which, being derived from *dwita* duality, by affixing the privative *a* is the opposite of *dwiatam*, the term usually applied to the belief that admits of more than one first cause: it is impossible to say when it was first revealed, yet, among various conjectures, the probability is that, the revelation of this faith is to be ascribed to Brahma, the creating power alone, and that it is as ancient, therefore, as the existence of the world.

People of limited understanding, not being able to comprehend the system of worshipping the Invisible being, have adopted doctrines and by that means confounded weak minds in remote times, but due punishment was inflicted on those Heretics, and Religion was very well established throughout India by the Reverend SENKARACHARYAM and his Disciples, who, however, did not pretend to *reform or discover* them or assume the title of a *reformer* or *discoverer.*

There are an immense number of books namely Vedas, Sastras, Puranas Agams, Tantras-Sutras, and Itihas, besides numerous commentaries compiled by many famous Theologians, both of ancient and modern times, respecting the doctrine of the worship of the Invisible Being. They are not only written in Sanscrit, but rendered into Pracruta, Tenugu, Tamil, Guzerat, Hindoostani, Maratta, Canari, &c. languages and immemorially studied by a great part of the Hindu Nation attached to the Adwaitam faith, and so our ancestors left no room to any person to make "*discoveries*" on the subject, or "to *proceed with unremitting exertion in the laudable work of* "*enlightening his countrymen and reclaiming* "*them from their debasing system of Idolatry*"

From my stating these doctrines to have been anciently translated, I beg it may not be construed that those translations are universally admitted—On the contrary, they are rejected by some and admitted by others for reason recited as follows:—

1st.—If the reader of them doubts the truth of the principles explained in the translation, the divine knowledge he acquired by them, becomes a doubtful faith, and that doubt cannot be removed unless he compare them with the original work, in that case the knowledge he lastly acquired becomes superior, and his study in the first instance becomes useless, and the cause of repeating the same work.

2nd.—Reading the Scriptures in the vulgar languages is prohibited by the Puranas.

3d.—These translations are omitted by others as useful and interesting in general, and particularly to those who have not sufficient knowledge in Sanscrit.

Not wishing to trouble my readers with the observations necessary to reconcile these three controversial points, I think it proper to leave it to them to judge which of them is admissible.

The Sútra Bhashyam, or the Commentary on the Theological Sutrams of Veda Vyasa, and those on the Uponishets &c. are in this part of India, constantly read and taught by the Bhramins all over the Country. Lectures and Themes are delivered in the various audiences frequently and purposely held by the Rajahs, Pundits and other respectable men in the Country. The ascribing of the "*discovery*" of a religious tenet so well known and celebrated, to a learned Native, cannot therefore, be here admitted by a Hindu, and he will not be more astonished at it, than he would at eahring that a man had one head and two eyes.

Previously to my proceeding to make any observations respecting Idolatrous Worship, I think it proper to state how the supreme Being is defined.

The Vedas Purans, &c. say that, this Being is infinite, eternal, self-intelligent, indivisible, inconsumable, pervading, universal, inconceivable, invisible, unalterable, and almighty. It is not subject either to the mind or senses. The translation of the following Sanscrit Slokams will serve to form an idea of its nature.

" He is eternal, he is the splendor of splendor,"
" He is supreme and glorious."

" The sun shines not with respect to him, nor
" the moon nor fire."

" Thou hearest without ears,"
" Thou smellest without a nose,"
" Thou walkest without legs."
" Thou seest without eyes,"
" Thou tastest without a tongue."

" Thou hast no gotram, nor birth, nor name, " nor shape, nor state nor place."

" Though thou art thus, yet thou art the Lord " of the Earth and the Heaven."

" In the same manner as the illusive appearance " of water, produced by the reflection of the rays " in the mirage."

" So the universe shines in thee, the real and " intelligent spirit."

" Thou canst not be known either by the Organs " or by the mind, as thou art self-resplendent and " distinct from elemental Being..'

" If ignorance be annihiliated by knowledge, as " darkness by the dawn, thy light will shine like " the sun."

" The whole had its birth in thee,"

" The whole rests in thee."

" The whole obtains its destruction in thee like " bubbles iu water,"

The difficulty of attaining the knowledge of this invisible and Almighty Spirit, is evident from the preceding verses, and all the Scriptures and other Authorities affirm that, the Soul, propelled by MAYA towards external objects and obscured by the ignorance of individuality, cannot obtain Mocaham (Salvation) unless it is freed from every impression either of vice and virtue, the illusions of MAYA; and until that time, it will continue to undergo various transmigrations and partake of misery and happiness, the result of its vices and virtues, in the terrestial, celestial and infernal worlds.

The eating food, slumbering, fear, love, and other animal functions and propensities, are common and natural both to the human and brute creation; they both seek for food and are subject to slumber. Out of the fear of death, &c. they either attack or fly when opposed by an enemy, but though the intellectual, powers of both races are the same in general and entirely directed towards external objects, yet one human race is endowed with the powers of reason and determination. These, if applied, serve to reason—who is himself? from whence he is come? what is the connection between him and the Supreme Being? how the Spirit in him is illusively inspired, and illusively beheld, and illusively divided from the pervading Spirit.

The mental powers of every Corporeal Being are, from the time of it's birth, attracted by external objects and they cannot be inverted towards the individual Spirit, or the object meant by the word "I," without great labour, practice, mental exercise, purification and the divine assistance, or favoring grace, of the Deity, without which a complete knowledge, of his Atmá or Spirit cannot be obtained.

It is said in the Scripture that the person void of this knowledge does not only remain self-ignorant, but it is decreed by the authorities tha he is a self-deceiver, and his ignorance finally proves fatal to himself.

In order to save the human race from the utter destruction occasioned by self-ignorance, Brahámá delivered the divine precepts in the Védas, both for the use of men of enlightened and limitted understanding. These precepts are divided into two parts, namely, Carmocándam, or works, and Gnanacandam, or knowledge, or faith, as European writers express it; these words I understand to mean essentially the same thing, for what is faith without adequacy of knowledge?

The first prescribes the mode of performing Yagam or Sacrifice, bestowing Danam or Alms, treats of penance, fasting, and of worshipping the Incarnations, in which the Supreme Deity has appeared on the earth for divine purposes. The ceremonies performed according to these modes, forsaking their fruits, are affirmed by the Védas to be mental exercises and mental purifications, necessary to obtain the knowledge of the divine nature.

The latter part treats on Theology, and Metaphysics, on the nature of spirit, of mental abstraction, the subjugation of the passions, &c. the meaning of which the Student must attain by reasoning, and must impress it well on the understanding by reflection; he must behold the Supreme Spirit alike in all things, he must constantly contemplate the union of his own Atmá, or Soul, with the Universal Supreme Spirit, which he must consider unconnected though in all connections and inactive in all things in action, and must comprehend the whole universe in him alone. The Gnani or the Man that has attained divine knowledge in this manner, should be unaffected in all his actions, the same in praise and insult, in friendship, and in enmity, in honor and dishonour, in pleasure and pain, in cold and heat; all his passions should be subdued, and his mind constantly fixed and united with the universal Spirit.

I must here introduce another extract from the publication to which I have referred—" we understand that on all the great Hindoo Festivals, "the *Friendly Society*, established by him, holds "meetings not only with the view that its mem"bers may keep aloof from the idolatrous ce"remonies of their countrymen, but, also, to re"new and strengthen their own faith in the "purer doctrines which they affirm to be esta"blished in the Veds. At these meetings they "have music and dancing, as well as their more "superstitious brethren ; but the songs are all "expressive of the peculiar tenets of the Mo"notheists."

It is evident from what is said above of the precepts in the Védam, that divine kuowledge cannot be obtained without purifying the soul, and such purification cannot take place without performing Yagams, bestowing Danams, by penance, worship, reading Theology and comprehending and reasoning on its meaning, but the *holding of meetings, playing music, singing songs and dancing*, which are ranked among carnal pleasures, are not ordained by scripture as mental purification.

It may be asked why purification cannot be attained by these songs, music, &c. since they are all intended to be expressive of the tenets of Monotheism? I answer that the completion of every undertaking in the world must take place by its respective means, for example the thirst must be quenched by water, milk and such like, but not with sand. These, the aforesaid means for quenching thirst, are known by human experience and usage, but the means to purify the unknown and invisible powers of the intellect cannot be ascertained by human understanding but by the precepts revealed by divine wisdom. Therefore, the setting aside the proper means such as Yagam, penance, worship, &c. and substituting dancing, music, and songs, appear in no way preferable by any doctrine.

[What has hitherto been said, applies only to the observations of the writer in the Calcutta Paper, for which Ram Mohun Roy cannot be answerable; I must, however, make a few remarks on the "Introduction" as it is stated to be, to his "trnas-

" lation of one of the chapters of the Sama " Veda." The author states that it is "a general characteristic of each Ved, that " the primary " chapters of each branch, treat of astronomy, " medicine, arms, and other arts and sciencs." All the Brahmans in this part of the Peninsula are studying the same Vedams as are read in the other part of the country, but I do not recollect to have read or heard of one treating on astronomy, medicine, or arms: the first is indeed an Angan of the Vedam, but the two latter are taught in separate Sastras.

The author continues—" they also exhibit " allegorical representation of the attributes " of the Supreme Being by means of earthly ob- " jects, &c." he then proceeds to state that the worship of these, as explained in the Veds, was " inculcated only for the sake of those whose " limitted understandings rendered them inca- " pable of comprehending and adoring the invi- " sible Supreme Being:" he does not appear satisfied, however, with this explanation; he seems to think it may not be thought sufficient to reconcile the doctrines of the two portions of the Veds, and he admits, that, if it is not— "the whole work must," "not only be stripped of its authority, but looked upon as altogether unintelligible." To say the least of this passage, RAM MOHUN ROY appears quite as willing to abandon as to defend the Scripture of his religion: but let us examine if it be necessary to abandon them so readily.

The attributes in the preceeding extract are affirmed by the Vedas to be the creating protecting, destroying and the like powers or incarnations of the Supreme Being—Their worship, under various representations, by means of consecrated objects, is prescribed by the scripture to the human race by way of mental exercise, who owing to the waving nature of their minds cannot, without assistance, fix their thoughts on the incomprehensible and Almighty Being.—Though the representations of the attributes are allegorical, yet the pervading nature of the

Supreme Being in the attributes, in their representations and in the objects dedicated to them, is not allegorical, and I regard the same as an ether diffused throughout ten thousand objects. If this reasoning be admitted, why cannot the prayer offered to the All-pervading Spirit in the dedicated object be considered as prayer to the universal and ALMIGHTY GOD?—If one part of the ocean be adored, the whole ocean is adored.

If a person be desirous to visit an Earthly Prince, he ought to be introduced, in the first instance, by his Ministers, but not of himself to rush in upon him at once regardless of offending him:—Should a Man wish to ascend a flight of stairs, he ought to proceed step by step and not to leap up several at a time so as to endanger the wounding of his legs; in like manner the grace of GOD ought to be obtained by degrees through the worship of his attributes.

I have further to observe, by way of example, that, although the milk pervades the whole body of a Cow, yet it is to be drawn only from the Teats; so though the Supreme Being pervades all, yet his mercy is obtained through the worship of his attributes to which a special energy is ascribed by the Scripture.—The worshippers are assured by the Vedás that the particular energy inherent in the attributes will crown their wishes, provided their zeal and their faith be unaltered and steady.

The objections to worshipping the attributes are not satisfactorily stated by the Author, but it seems that it is his general idea that it is not a worship directly to the Supreme Being, and that it is not prescribed in the Scriptures of certain nations: as to the last objection it is clear, however, that the worship of the attributes is not merely not rejected, but prescribed by the Scriptures of our religion; here is the difference, and, as the deliverers of the Scripture, of any religion are not of a nature to be seen or spoken to for the purpose of proving their avidity, the truth of either opinion, can only be established by analogy, inference, and other modes of logic.

If the worship of the attributes be rejected, what means can be substituted to inculcate the truth and to enlighten the understanding of an indolent man, who on being told that the God is all-pervading and invisible, thinks him to be like the air, or the sky; or hearing that, by a figure of speech, he is called the splendor of splendor, believes that he is of a luminous nature? If these helps be denied him, will he not at last become ignorant of the true faith, or be induced to follow atheistical doctrines, rather than to trouble his head to attain the difficult knowledge of the divine nature?

I have lastly to observe that, according to the Christian Doctrine of the Trinity, or the three persons in the Godhead, though one and united yet are personally, or occasionably, distinguished, and prayers offered to the Godhead are concluded by the words "through Jesus Christ our

Saviour." I believe, though I may be mistaken, that the Saviour should be considered a personification of the mercy and kindness of God (I mean actual, not allegorical personification; pure allegory I leave to Ram Mohun Roy)—if this be so, is not mercy an attribute of God? Is not the prayer offered to him, through his attribute, of the same nature as the worship of the Hindus? Do not the votaries of the Christian Religion, like the Hindus, acknowledge him to be essentially united to the Godhead, though occasionally separate, and do they not believe that they are certain of obtaining salvation in this faith?

For these reasons, why cannot the Hindu Worship of the attributes, which are affirmed to be essentially united, but occasionally separate from the Godhead, be admitted and why may not this be the means of obtaining Mocsham or Salvation? It seems upon the whole that technical terms, modes of worship, and external rights, respectively observed, constitute an apparent difference between the religions of the Earth, though in truth there be none.

I am, Sir

Your most obedient humble servant,

B. SENKARA SASTRI,

IId. English Master in the College of Fort St. George.

Madras, 26th December, 1816.

Before I attempt to reply to the observations, that the learned gentleman, who signs himself Senkara Sastri, has offered in his letter of the 20th December last, addressed to the Editor of the Madras Courier, on the subject of an article, published in the Calcutta Gazette, and on my translation of an abridgment of the Vedanta and of the two chapters of the Vedas; I beg to be allowed to express the disappointment I have felt, in receiving from a learned Brahman, controversial remarks on Hindoo Theology, written in a foreign language; as it is the invariable practice of the natives of all Provinces of Hindoostan, to hold their discussions on such subjects, in Sangscrit, which is the learned language common to all of them, and in which they may naturally be expected to convey their ideas, with perfect correctness, and greater facility than in any foreign tongue: Nor need it be alleged that, by adopting this established channel of controversy, the opportunity of appealing to public opinion on the subject must be lost; as a subsequent translation from the Sungscrit into English may sufficiently serve that purpose. The irregularity of this mode of proceeding however, gives me room to suspect that the letter in question, is the production of the pen of an English Gentleman, whose liberality *I suppose*, has induced him to attempt an apology, even for the absurd idolatry of his fellow-creatures. If this inference be correct, while I congratulate that Gentleman on his progress in a knowledge of the sublime doctrines of the Vedanta, I must, at the same time, take the liberty of entreating that he will for the future, prefer consulting the original works written upon those doctrines, to relying on the second-hand information on the subject, that may be offered him by any person whatsoever.

The learned Gentleman commences by objecting to the terms *discoverer* and *reformer*, in which the Editor of the Calcutta Gazette was pleased to make mention of me. He states "that Peo-"ple of limited understanding, not being able

" to comprehend the system of worshipping the
" invisible Being, have adopted false doctrines
" and by that means confounded weak minds
" in remote times, but due punishment was in-
" flicted on those Heretics, and religion was
" very well established throughout India by
" the Reverend Sankaracharja and his disci-
" ples, who, however, did not pretend to *reform*
" or *discover* them or assume the title of a *reformer* or *discoverer*." In none of my writings, nor in any verbal discussion, have I ever pretended to reform or to discover the doctrines of the unity of God, nor have I ever assumed the title of reformer or discoverer: so far from such an assumption, I have urged in every work that I have hitherto published, that the doctrines of the unity of God are real Hindooism, as that religion was practised by our ancestors, and as it is well known even at the present age to many learned Brahmins: I beg to repeat a few of the passages to which I allude.

In the introduction to the abridgment of the Vedanta I have said "In order, therefore, "to vindicate my own faith and that of *our* "*forefathers,* I have been endeavouring, for "some time past, to convince my countrymen "of the *true meaning of our sacred* books: "and prove that my aberration deserves not the "opprobrium, which some unreflecting persons "have been so ready to throw upon me" In another place of the same introduction. "The "present is an endeavour to render an abridg-"ment of the same (the Vedanta) into English, "by which I expect to prove to my European "friends, that the superstitious practices, which "deform the Hindoo religion, have nothing to "do with the pure spirit of its dictates." In the introduction of the Cenopanishad. "This "work will, I trust, by explaining to my coun-"trymen *the real spirit of the Hindoo scrip-"tures, which is but the declaration of the "unity of God,* tend in a great degree to cor-"rect the erroneous conceptions, which have

" prevailed with regard to the doctrines they inculcate:" and in the Preface of the Ishopa-" nished, *many learned Brahmins* are perfect-" ly aware of the absurdity of idol worship, and *are well informed of the nature of the pure mode of divine worship.*" A reconsideration of these passages will, I hope, convince the learned Gentleman, that I never advanced any claim to the title either of a reformer, or of a discoverer of the doctrines of the unity of the Godhead— It is not at all impossible that from the perusal of the Translations above alluded to, the Editor of the Calcutta Gazette, finding the system of idolatry into which Hindoos are now completely sunk, quite inconsistent with the real spirit of their scriptures, may have imagined that their contents had become entirely forgotten and unknown; and that I was the first to point out the absurdity of idol worship and to inculcate the propriety of the pure divine worship, ordained by their vedas, their Smrits and their Poorans. From this idea, and from finding in his intercourse with other Hindoos, that I was stigmatised by many, however unjustly, as an *innovator*, he may have been, not unnaturally, misled to apply to me the epithets of discoverer and reformer.

2ndly. The learned Gentleman states "There "are an immense number of Books, namely, *Ve*-"*das*, Sastras, Poorans, Agams, Tantras, Sutras "and Itihas, besides numerous commentaries "compiled by many famous Theologians, both "of ancient and modern times, respecting the "doctrines of the worship of the invisible being. "They are not only written in Sangscrit but ren-"dered into the Pracreta, Tenuga, Tamol, Gujrate, "Hindoostani, Marhutta, and Canari languages, and "immemorialy studied by a great part of the "Hindu nation, attached to the adwaitum faith "&c." This statement of the learned Gentleman, as far as it is correct, corroborates indeed my assertion, with respect to the doctrines of the worship of the invisible Supreme spirit, being unanimously inculcated by all the Hindoo Sastras; and naturally leads to severe reflections on the selfishness which must actuate those Bramionical teachers who, notwithstanding the unanimous authority of the Sastras, for the adoption of pure worship, yet, with the view of maintaining the title of God which they arrogate to themselves, and of deriving pecuniary and other advantages from the numerous rites and festivals of idol worship, constantly advance and encourage idolatry to the utmost of their power. I must remark, however, that, there is no translation of the vedas into any of the modern languages of Hindoostan with which I am acquainted, and it is for that reason that I have translated into Bengali the vedanta, the Cenopanishad of the Sama veda, Ishopanishad of the Yojur veda, &c. with the contents of which none but the learned among my countrymen were at all acquainted.

3rdly. The learned Gentleman states that, the translations of the scripture into the vulgar language, are rejected by some people; and he assigns as reasons for their so doing that, "if the "reader of them doubts the truth of the princi-

"ples explained in the translation, the divine "knowledge he acquired by them, becomes a "doubtful faith and that doubt cannot be re-"moved unless he compare them with the ori-"ginal work: In that case the knowledge he "lastly acquired becomes superior, and his study in "the first instance becomes useless and the cause of "repeating the same work." When a translation of a work written in a foreign tongue is made by a person at all acquainted with that language into his native tongue, and the same translation is sanctioned and approved of by many natives of the same Country who are perfectly conversant with that foreign language; the translation I presume may be received with confidence as a satisfactory interpretation of the original work; both by the vulgar and by men of literature.

It must not be supposed, however, that I am inclined to assert that, there is not the least room to doubt the accuracy of such a translation; because the meaning of authors, even in the original works is very frequently dubious, especially in a language like Sungscrit; every sentence of which almost, admits of being explained in different senses—But should the possibility of errors in every translation be admitted as reason for with-holding all confidence in their contents, such a rule would shake our belief, not only in the principles explained in the translation of the vedant into the current language, but also in all information respecting foreign History and theology, obtained by means of translations: In that case we must either learn all the languages that are spoken by the different nations in the world, to acquire a knowledge of their Histories and religions, or be content to know nothing of any Country besides our own. The second reason which the learned Gentleman assigns for their objection to the translation is, that "Reading the scripture in "the vulgar languages is prohibited by the Poorans." I have not yet met with any texts of any Poorans which prohibit the explanation of the scriptures in the vulgar tongue; on the contrary the Poorans allow that practice very frequently. I repeat one of these declarations from the Shiva Dhurma, quoted by the great Bughnund. "He who can interpret, according to "the ratio of the understanding of his pupils, thro' "Sunscrit, or thro' the vulgar languages, or by "means of the current language of the Coun- "try, is entitled, spiritual father." Moreover in every part of Hindoostan all professors of the Sungscrit language instructing beginners in the veds, Poorans, and in other sastras, interpret them in the vulgar languages; especially spiritual fathers in exposition of those parts of he veds and Poorans, which allegorically introduce a plurality of Gods and idol-worship; doctrines which tend so much to their own worldly advantage.

The learned Gentleman states that, "The first "of the veda prescribes the mode of performing "yagam or sacrifice, bestowing daneem or alms, "treats of penance, fasting and of worshipping, "the incarnations, in which the supreme Deity "has appeared on the Earth for divine purposes.

"The ceremonies performed according to these "modes, forsaking their fruits, are affirmed by "the vedas to be mental exercises and mental "purifications necessary to obtain the knowledge "of the divine nature." I, in common with the vedas and the vedant, and Munoo (the first and best of Hindoo *Lawgivers*) as well as with the most celebrated Sankaracharga, deny these ceremonies being necessary to obtain the knowledge of the divine nature; as the vedant positively declares in text 36th Sec. 4th Chap: 3rd "Man may acquire "the true knowledge of God even without ob- "serving the rules and rites prescribed by the ved "for each class; as it is found in the ved that "many persons, who neglected the performance "of the rites and ceremonies, owing to their per- "petual attention to the adoration of the supreme "being, acquired the true knowledge respecting the "supreme spirit." The ved says "Many learned "true Believers never worshipped fire or any celes- "tial Gods through fire." And also the vedant asserts in the 1st text of 3rd Sec. of the 3rd chap. "The worship authorized by all the veds is one, "as the directions for the worship of the only "supreme being are invariably found in the "Ved, and the epithets of the supreme and "omnipresent being &c. commonly imply God "alone." Munoo as I have elsewhere quoted, thus declares on the same point chap. 12th text 92nd "Thus must the chief of "the twice born, tho' he neglect the ceremonial "rites mentioned in the sastra, be diligent in "attaining a knowledge of God, in controling "his organs of sense and in repeating the ved." Again chapter 4th text 23rd "some constantly sa-"crifice their breath in their speech, *when they in-"struct others of God aloud* and their speech in their "breath, *when they meditate in silence* perceiving "in their speech and breath thus employed the "imperishable fruit of a sacrificial offering 24th." "Other Brahmans incessantly perform those sa-"crifices only; seeing with the Eye of divine "learning that the scriptural knowledge is the

" root of every ceremonial observance." And also the same author declares in the chap. 2nd text 84. " All rites ordained in the veda, oblations " to Fire and solemn sacrifices, pass away ; but " that, which passes not away is declared to be " the syllable om, thence called acshora ; since " it is a symbol of God, the Lord of created " Beings "

5*thly.* The learned Gentleman states that, " The " difficulty of attaining a knowledge of the in-" visible and almighty spirit is evident from the " preceding verses." I agree with him in that point ; that the attainment of perfect knowledge of the nature of the Godhead is certainly difficult or rather impossible ; but to read the existence of the almighty being, in his works of nature is not, I will dare to say, so difficult to the mind of a man possessed of common sense and unfettered by prejudice, as to conceive artificial images to be possessed, at once, of the opposite natures of human and divine Beings, which idolaters constantly ascribe to their idols ;—strangely believing that things so *constructed* can be converted by ceremonies into *constructors* of the universe.

6thly The learned Gentleman objects to our introducing songs, altho' expressing only the peculiar tenets of monotheism, and says.

" But the holding of meetings, playing music, " singing songs, and dancing, which are ranked " among carnal pleasures, are not ordained by " scripture as mental purification." The practice of dancing in divine worship, I agree, is not ordained by the scripture, and accordingly never was introduced in our worship: any mention of dancing in the Calcutta Gazette must, therefore, have proceeded from misinformation of the Editor. But respecting the propriety of introducing monotheistical songs in the divine worship, I beg leave to refer the Gentleman to the text 114th and 115th of the 3rd chapter of Yagnyavalca, who authorizes not only scriptural music in divine contemplation, but also the songs that are composed by the vulgar. It is also evident that any interesting idea is calculated to make more impression upon the mind, when conveyed in musical verses, than when delivered in the form of common conversation.

7thly. The learned Gentleman says "All the "Bhramins in this Peninsula are studying the "same vedom as are read in the other parts of "the Country; but I do not recollect to have read "or heard of one treating on astromony, me-"dicine or arms: the first is indeed an ongam "of the vedam, but the two latter are taught "in separate sastras." In answer to which I beg to be allowed to refer the Gentleman to the following text of the Nervan. "The veds while "talking of Planets, botany, austere duties, arms "rites, natural consequences, and several other "subjects, are purified by the inculcation of the "doctrines of the supreme spirit." And also to the latter end of the Mahanervana agam.

From the perusal of these texts, I trust, he will be convinced that, vedas not only treat of Astronomy, Medicine and arms, but also of morality and natural Philosophy, and that all arts and sciences that are treated of in othersastras, were originally introduced by the veds, see also Munoo, chapter 12 verses 97 and 98. I cannot of course be expected to be answerable for Bruhmans neglecting entirely the study of the scientific parts of the ved, and putting in practice, and promulgating to the utmost of their power, that part of them which, treating of rites and festivals, is justly considered as the source of their worldly advantages and support of their alledged divinity.

8thly I observe, that on the following statement in my introduction to the Cenopunished viz. "should this explanation given by the ved itself "as well as by its celebrated commentators vyas "not be allowed to reconcile these passages which "are seemingly at variance with each other, as "those that declare the unity of the invisible "supreme being, with others which describe a "plurality of independent visible Gods, the whole "work must I am afraid not only be stripped of "its authority but looked upon as altogether "unintelligible," the learned Gentleman has remarked that "To say the least of this passage "RAM MOHUN ROY appears quite as willing to "abandon as to defend the scripture of his "Religion."

In the foregoing paragraph, however, I did no more than logically confine the case to two points viz. that the explanation of the ved and of its commentators must either be admitted as sufficiently reconciling the apparent contradictions between different passages of the ved, or must not be admitted. In the latter case the ved must necessarily be supposed to be inconsistent with itself, and therefore altogether unintelligible, which is directly contrary to the faith of Hindoos of every discription; consequently they must admit that those explanations do sufficiently reconcile the seeming contradictions between the chapters of the vedas.

9*thly*. The learned Gentleman says that "Their "(the attributes and incarnations) worship under

" various representations by means of consecrated " objects, is prescribed by the scripture to the " human race by way of mental exercises &c." I cannot admit that the worship of these attributes under various representations by means of consecrated objects, has been prescribed by the Ved to the HUMAN RACE; as this kind of worship of consecrated objects is enjoined by the Sastra to those only, who are incapable of raising their minds to the notion of an invisible supreme Being. I have quoted several authorities for this assertion in my Preface to the Ishopanishad, and beg to repeat here one or two of them. " The vulgar look " for their God in water, men of more extended " knowledge in celestial bodies; the ignorant " in wood, bricks and stones; but learned men " in the universal soul." " Thus corresponding " to the nature of different Powers or qualities, " numerous figures have been invented for the " benefit of those, *who are not possessed of suffi-* " *cient understanding.*" Permit me in this instance to ask, whether every Mussulman in Turkey and Arabia, from the highest to the lowest, every Protestant christian at least of Europe, and many followers of Cabeer and Nanuck, do worship God without the assistance of consecrated objects? If so, how can we suppose that the human race is not capable of adoring the supreme Being without the puerile practice of having recourse to visible objects.

10*thly*. The learned Gentleman is of opinion that, the attributes of God exist distinctly from God; and he compares the relation between God and those attributes to that of a King to his ministers, as he says,

"If a person be desirous to visit an earthly "Prince, he ought to be introduced in the "first instance by his Ministers &c.." and "In "like manner the Grace of God ought to be "obtained by the grace through the worship "of his attributes." This opinion I am extremely sorry to find, is directly contrary to all the Vedant doctrines interpreted to us by the most revered Sankaracharjya, which are real adwaita or non-duality: they affirm that God has no second that may be possessed of eternal existence, either of the same nature with himself or of a different nature from him, nor any second of that nature that might be called either his part or his *quality*. The 16th Text of the 2nd Section of 3rd Chap: " The Ved has de-" clared the Supreme Being to be mere under-" standing." The Ved says " God is real " existence, wisdom and eternity:" The Ved very often calls the supreme existence by the epithets of existent, wise and eternal; and assigns as the reason for adopting such epithets, that the Ved in the first instance speaks of God according to human idea, which views quality separately from person, in order to facilitate our comprehension of objects. In case these attributes should be supposed, as the learned Gentleman asserts, to be separate existences, it necessarily follows, that they must be either eternal or non-eternal: The former case viz. the existence of a plurality of beings imbued like

God himself with the property of eternal duration, strikes immediately at the root of all the doctrines relative to the unity of the supreme being contained in the vedant. By the latter sentiment, namely that the power and attributes of God are not eternal, we are led at once into the belief that the nature of God is susceptible of change, and consequently that he is not eternal, which makes no inconsiderable step toward atheisim itself. These are the obvious and dangerous consequences, resulting from the learned Gentleman's doctrine that the attributes of the supreme Being are distinct existences. I am quite at a loss to know how these attributes of the pure and perfect supreme being, (as the learned Gentleman declares them to exist really and separately, and not fictitiously and allegorically) can be so sensual and destitute of morality, as the creating attribute or Brahma is said to be, by the Poorans; which represent him in one instance, as attempting to commit a rape upon his own daughter: The Protecting attribute or Vishnu, is in another place affirmed to have fraudulently violated the chastity of Brinda, in order to kill her husband. Shiva, the destroying attribute, is said to have had a criminal attachment to Moheni, disregarding all ideas of decency. And a thousand similar examples must be familiar to every reader of the Poorans. I should be obliged by the learned Gentleman's shewing, how the contemplation of such circumstances, which are constantly related by the worshippers of these attributes even in their sermons, can be instrumental towards the purification of the mind, conducive to morality and productive of eternal beatitude. Besides, though the learned Gentleman in this instance considers these attributes to be separate existences, yet in another place he seems to view them as parts of the Supreme Being; as he says, "If one "part of the ocean be adored, the ocean is "adored." I am somewhat at a loss to understand, how the learned Gentleman proposes to reconcile this apparent contradiction. I must observe, however, in this place, that the comparison drawn between the relation of God and those attributes, and that of a King and his Ministers, is totally inconsistent with the faith entertained by Hindoos of the present day; who so far from considering these objects of worship as mere instruments by which they may arrive at the power of contemplating the God of nature, regard them in the light of independent Gods, to each of whom, however absurdly, they attribute almighty power, and a claim to worship, solely on his own account.

11*thly*. The learned Gentleman is dissatisfied with the objection mentioned in my translation to worshiping these fictitious representations; and remarks that, "The objections to worshipping the attributes "are not satisfactorily stated by the author." I consequently repeat the following authorities which I hope may answer my purpose. The folloing are the declarations of the ved: "He, who worships any God "exceping the supreme Being, and thinks that he "himself is distinct and inferior to that God,

"knows nothing, and is considered as a domes-"
"tic beast of these Gods." "A state even so"
"high as that of Brahma does not afford real"
"bless." "Adore God alone." "None but"
"the supreme being is to be worshipped; nothing"
"excepting him should be adored by a wise man."
I repeat also the following texts of the vedant:
"The declaration of the Ved that, those that wor-"
"ship the celestial Gods are the food of such Gods,"
"is an allegorical expression, and only means"
"that they are comforts to the celestial Gods,"
"as food to mankind; for he who has no faith"
"in the supreme Being is rendered subject to"
"these Gods. The Ved affirms the same."

And the revered Sankaracharjya has frequently declared the state of celestial Gods to be that of demons, in the Bhasya of the Ishopanishad and of others.

To these authorities a thousand others might be added. But should the learned Gentleman require some practical grounds for objecting to the idolatrous worship of the Hindoos,

I can be at no loss to give him numberless instances, where the ceremonies that have been instituted under the pretext of honoring the all perfect author of nature, are of a tendency utterly subversive of every moral principle.

I begin with Krishna as the most adored of all the Incarnations, the number of whose devotees is exceedingly great. His worship is made to consist in the institution of his image or picture, accompanied by one or more females, and in the contemplation of his history and behaviour, such as his perpetration of murder upon a female of the name of Pootna; his compelling great number of married and unmarried women to stand before him denuded, his debauching them and several others, to the mortal affliction of their husbands and relations, his annoying them, by violating the laws of cleanliness and other facts of the same nature: The grossness of his worship does not find a limit here. His devotees very often personify (in the same manner as European actors upon stages do) him and his female companions, dancing with indecent gestures and singing songs, relative to his love and debaucheries. It it impossible to explain in language fit to meet the public eye, the mode in which Muhadéva, or the destroying attribute, is worshipped by the generality of the Hindoos. Suffice it to say that, it is altogether congenial with the iudecent nature of the Image, under whose form he is most commonly adored.

The stories respecting him, which are read by his devotees in the Tuntras, are of a nature that if told of any man, would be offensive to the ears of the most abandoned of either sex. In the worship of Kali, human sacrifices, the use of wine, criminal intercourse and licentious songs are included: the first of these practices has become generally extinct; but it is believed that there are parts of the country where human victims are still offered.

Debaucheery, however, universally forms the principle part of the worship of her followers Nigam and other Tantras may satisfy every reader of the horrible tenets of the worshippers of the two latter deities. The modes of worship of almost all the inferior dieties are pretty much the same. Having so far explained the nature of worship adopted by Hindoos in general for the propitiation of their allegorical attributes in direct opposition to the mode of pure divine worship inculcated by the vedas, I cannot but entertain a strong hope that the learned Gentleman, who ranks even monotheisticalsongs among carnal pleasures, and consequently rejects their admittance in worship, will no longer stand forward as an advocate for the worship of separate and independent at tributes and Incarnations.

12*thly*. The learned Gentleman says " That the saviour" meaning Christ, " shonld be considered a personification of the Mercy and kindness of God (I mean actual not allegorical personification :)" From the little knowledge I had acquired of the tenets of christians and those of antichristians, I thought their were only three prevailing opinions respecting the nature of Christ viz. That he was considered by some as the expounder of the laws of God, and the mediator between God and man ; by many to be one of the three mysterious persons of the Godhead ; whilst others, such as the Jews, say that, he was a mere man. But to consider Christ as a personification of the mercy of God is, if I mistake not, a new doctrine in Christianity, the discussion of which, however, has no connection with the present subject. I however must observe that this opinion, which the learned Gentleman has formed of Christ being a personification of the mercy of God, is similar to that entertained by Mussulmans, for a period of upwards of a thousand years, respecting Mohummud, whom they call mercy of God upon all his creatures. The learned Gentleman in the conclusion of his observations has left, as he says, the doctrines of pure allegory to me. It would have been more consistent with Justice, had he left pure allegory also to the veds, which declare "appellations and figures of all kinds "are innovations." and which have allegorically represented God in the figure of the universe: "Fire is his head, the sun and the moon are his two eyes &c." and which have also represented all human internal qualities by different earthly objects, and also to Vyas, who has strictly followed the veds in these figurative representations, and to Sankaracharjya, who also adopted the mode of allegory, in his Bhashya of the vedant and of the upanishadas.

POSTSCRIPT.

Since printing the foregoing observations, I happened to peruse, with the greatest degree of satisfaction, a letter written by a Gentleman, who signs himself Alexipharmicus, to the Editor of the Madras Courier under date the 13th of January last, in reply to the arguments adduced by Sankara Sastri in support of idolatry.

The compassion which the gentleman feels towards an unfortunate but large body of his fellow-creatures, the Inhabitants of India, has induced him not only to abstain from remaining neuter on the subject, but to come forward and refute every argument urged by Sankara Sastri in defence of Hindoo Paganism

I

—a system of Religion wherein suicide is reckoned one of the most meritorious acts, and human Victims, as well as dreadful and sanguinary torments, are considered as the sure means of propitiating their supposed Deities.

I must therefore beg leave, as in duty bound, to express the gratitude I feel, for the interest which the humane and liberal minded Gentleman has taken, in the welfare of my Countrymen.